EXPLORING NATURE

AMAZING SNAKES

An exciting insight into the weird and wonderful world of snakes and how they live, with 190 pictures • Barbara Taylor

Consultant: Michael Chinery

ARMADILLO

This edition is published by Armadillo, an imprint of Anness Publishing Ltd, Blaby Road, Wigston, Leicestershire LE18 4SE; info@anness.com

www.annesspublishing.com

Anness Publishing has a new picture agency outlet for images for publishing, promotions or advertising. Please visit our website www.practicalpictures.com for more information.

Publisher: Joanna Lorenz
Managing Editor: Sue Grabham
Senior Editor: Nicole Pearson
Editor: Nicky Barber
Illustrations: Julian Baker, David Webb
Designer: Simon Wilder
Production Controller: Pirong Wang

Special Photography: Kim Taylor/ Warren Photographic: pages 1, 2, 3, 4–5, 7tr, 10bl, 10bm, 11tr, 12–13, 14–15, 16ml, 16bl, 24–5, 27tr, 29t, 31bl, 34tl, 34–5, 35mr, 36bl, 47r, 52ml, 56tr, 57t, 58b, 59m, 59bl, 62, 63 and 64.
For other picture credits, see page 63.

Our special thanks to the following people for kindly allowing their snakes to be photographed: Mike Alexander, Jason Chippington and Graham Shred.

PUBLISHER'S NOTE
Although the advice and information in this book are believed to be accurate and true at the time of going to press, neither the authors nor the publisher can accept any legal responsibility or liability for any errors or omissions that may have been made.

No animals were harmed during the making of this book.

Manufacturer: Anness Publishing Ltd, Blaby Road, Wigston, Leicestershire LE18 4SE, England
For Product Tracking go to: www.annesspublishing.com/tracking
Batch: 6777-22412-1127

C O N

T E N T S

long, thin,
bendy body
with no legs

tough scales
protect the
body and
stop it
drying out

Snake Life

Snakes are a kind of reptile related
to lizards, crocodiles and turtles.
Altogether, there are about 2,700
different kinds of snake, but only 300
or so are able to kill people. In Europe or
North America, you are more likely to be
struck by lightning than to be bitten by a
venomous snake. All snakes have long bodies covered
with waterproof scales. They are flesh eaters and
swallow their prey whole. Snakes have always had
a special place in myths and legends, being used
as symbols of both good and evil.

◄ A SNAKE'S TAIL

The tail of a snake is the part behind a small opening
called the cloaca, where the body wastes pass out.
The snake narrows slightly where the
tail begins.

tail, the part
of the body
that tapers
off to a point

grass snake

◄ SNAKE HEADS

Most snakes have a definite head and neck.
But in some snakes, one end of the body looks
very much like the other end!

◄ FORKED TONGUES

Snakes and some lizards have forked tongues. A snake flicks its tongue to taste and smell the air. This gives the snake a picture of what is around it. A snake does this every few seconds if it is hunting or if there is any danger nearby.

rattlesnake
(*Crotalus*)

Colombian rainbow boa
(*Epicrates cenchria maurus*)

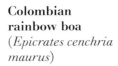

▲ SCALY SKIN

A covering of tough, dry scales grows out of a snake's skin. The scales usually hide the skin. After a big meal, the scaly skin stretches so that the skin becomes visible between the scales. A snake's scales protect its body while allowing it to stretch, coil and bend. The scales may be either rough or smooth.

red-tailed boa
(*Boa constrictor*)

Did you know? Snakes never feel slimy to the touch.

Medusa

An ancient Greek myth tells of Medusa, a monster with snakes for hair. Anyone who looked at her was turned to stone. Perseus managed to avoid this fate by using his polished shield to look only at the monster's reflection. He cut off Medusa's head and carried it home, dripping with blood. As each drop touched the earth, it turned into a snake.

Did you know? A boa squeezes its prey to death in its coils.

eye has no eyelid

forked tongue

Shapes and Sizes

Can you imagine a snake as tall as a three-storey house? The reticulated python is this big. The biggest snakes' bodies measure nearly 1m (3ft) round. Other snakes are as thin as a pencil and small enough to fit into the palm of your hand. Snakes also have different shapes to suit their environments. Sea snakes, for example, have flat bodies and tails like oars to help them push against the water and move forwards.

▼ THICK AND THIN

Vipers mostly have thick bodies with much thinner, short tails. The bags of venom on either side of a viper's head take up a lot of space, so the head is quite large.

rhinoceros viper
(*Bitis nasicornis*)

◄ LONG AND THIN

A tree snake's long, thin shape helps it to slide along leaves and branches. Even its head is long, pointed and very light so that it does not weigh the snake down as it reaches for the next branch.

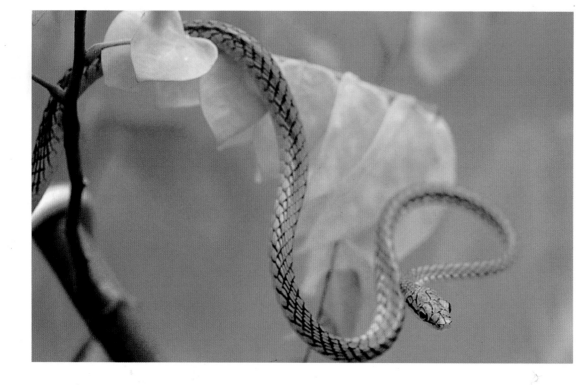

► BEING BIG

This picture shows the head of a red-tailed boa. The head measures about 15cm (6in). The red-tailed boa usually grows to an overall length of about 3.5m (13ft). The longest snake in the world is the reticulated python, which can grow up to 10m (32ft). Other giant snakes include the anaconda, other boas and the pythons.

Did you know? The blind snake, Leptotyphlops bilineata, is the shortest snake in the world at only 10.8cm (4¼in) long.

red-tailed boa
(Boa constrictor)

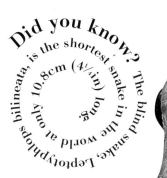

▲ SMALLEST SNAKE

The world's smallest snakes are the blind snakes and the thread snakes. These tiny creatures are less than 40cm (16in) long.

▼ SLENDER SNAKES

A harmless garter snake has a narrow head because it does not need space for bags of venom. Its body is slender and small – from 0.3m (1ft) to 1.2m (4ft) long.

garter snake
(*Thamnophis sirtalis*)

tree snake's long, thin body and pointed head

burrowing snake's small, thin body

viper's short, thick body

python's large, round body

▲ SNAKE SHAPES

Snakes have four general body shapes and lengths.

egg-eating snake (*Dasypeltis fasciata*)

◄ **STRETCHY STOMACH**
Luckily, the throat and gut of the egg-eating snake are so elastic that its thin body can stretch enough to swallow a whole egg. Muscles in the throat and first part of the gut help force food down into the stomach.

How Snakes Work

A snake has a stretched-out inside to match its long, thin outside. The backbone extends along the whole body with hundreds of ribs joined to it. There is not much room for organs such as the heart, lungs, kidneys and liver, so these organs are thin shapes to fit inside the snake's body. Many snakes have only one lung. The stomach and gut are stretchy so that they can hold large meals. When a snake swallows big prey, it pushes the opening of the windpipe up from the floor of the mouth in order to keep breathing. Snakes are cold-blooded, which means that their body temperature is the same as their surroundings.

right lung is very long and thin and does the work of two lungs

liver is very long and thin

flexible tail bone, which extends from the back bone

▼ **INSIDE A SNAKE**
This diagram shows the inside of a male snake. The organs are arranged to fit the snake's long shape. In most species, paired organs, such as the kidneys, are the same size and placed opposite each other.

▲ **COLD-BLOODED CREATURE**
Like all snakes, the banded rattlesnake is cold-blooded.

rectum through which waste is passed to the cloaca

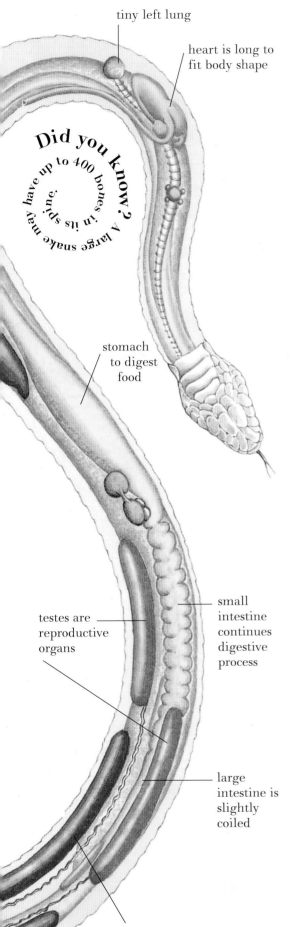

tiny left lung

heart is long to fit body shape

Did you know? A large snake may have up to 400 bones in its spine.

stomach to digest food

testes are reproductive organs

small intestine continues digestive process

large intestine is slightly coiled

kidneys process and recycle waste

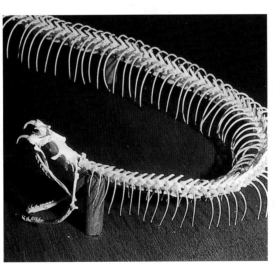

▲ SNAKE BONES

This X-ray of a grass snake shows the delicate bones that make up its skeleton. There are no arm, leg, shoulder or hip bones. The snake's ribs do not extend into the tail.

◄ SKELETON

A snake's skeleton is made up of a skull and a long backbone with ribs arching out from it. The free ends of the ribs are linked by muscles.

9

A Scaly Skin

A snake's scales are extra-thick pieces of skin. Like a hard shell, the scales protect the snake from knocks and scrapes as it moves. They also allow the skin to stretch when the snake moves or feeds. Scales are usually made of a horny substance, called keratin. Every part of a snake's body is covered by a layer of scales, including the eyes. The clear, bubble-like scale that protects each eye is called a brille or spectacle.

▼ HORNED SNAKE

As its name suggests, the European nose-horned viper has a strange horn on its nose. The horn is made up of small scales that lie over a bony or fleshy lump sticking out at the end of the nose.

nose-horned viper
(*Vipera ammodytes*)

▼ SCUTES

Most snakes have a row of broad scales, called scutes, underneath their bodies. The scutes go across a snake's body from side to side, and end where the tail starts. Scutes help snakes to grip the ground.

corn snake's scutes

▼ WARNING RATTLE

The rattlesnake has a number of hollow tail-tips that make a buzzing sound when shaken. The snake uses this sound to warn enemies. When it sheds its skin, a section at the end of the tail is left, adding another piece to the rattle.

rattlesnake's rattle

► SKIN SCALES

The scales of a snake grow out of the top layer of the skin, called the epidermis. There are different kinds of scales. Keeled scales may help snakes to grip surfaces, or break up a snake's outline for camouflage. Smooth scales make it easier for the snake to squeeze through tight spaces.

Look closely at the rough scales of the puff adder (left) and you will see a raised ridge, or keel, sticking up in the middle of each one.

Did you know? Most snakes get their patterns from pigments in the scales.

corn snake's scales

The wart snake (right) uses its scales to grip its food. Its rough scales help the snake to keep a firm hold on slippery fish until it can swallow them. The snake's scales do not overlap.

Eternal Youth

A poem written in the Middle East about 3,700 years ago tells a story about why snakes can shed their skins. The hero of the poem is Gilgamesh (shown here holding a captured lion). He finds a magic plant that will make a person young again. While he is washing at a pool, a snake eats the plant. Since then, snakes have been able to shed their skins and become young again. But people have never found the plant – which is why they always grow old and die.

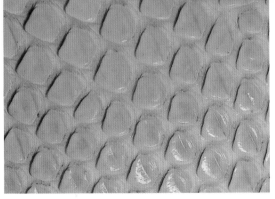

The green scales and stretched blue skin (left) belong to a boa. These smooth scales help the boa to slide over leafy branches. Burrowing snakes have smooth scales so that they can slip through soil.

Did you know? The hairy bush viper has pointed scales with curled tips, making it look hairy.

1 In the days before its skin peels, a snake is bad-tempered and sluggish, and it is dull in appearance. Its eyes turn cloudy as their coverings loosen. About a day before shedding, the eyes clear.

Focus on New Skin

About six times a year, an adult snake wriggles out of its old, tight skin to reveal a new, shiny skin underneath. Snakes shed their worn-out skin and scales in one piece. This process is called shedding or sloughing. Snakes only shed when a new layer of skin and scales has grown underneath the old skin. Adult snakes do this up to about six times a year.

2 The paper-thin layer of outer skin and scales first starts to peel away around the mouth. The snake rubs its jaws and chin against rocks or rough bark, and crawls through plants. This helps to push off the loose layer of skin.

Did you know? A baby snake may shed its skin when it is only a few days old.

12

3 The outer layer of skin gradually peels back from the head over the rest of the body. The snake slides out of its old skin, which comes off inside-out. It is rather like taking hold of a long sock at the top and peeling it down over your leg and foot!

Did you know? Female snakes often shed their skin just before giving birth.

4 A snake usually takes several hours to shed its whole skin. The old skin is moist and supple soon after shedding, but gradually dries out to become crinkly and rather brittle. The discarded skin is a copy of the snake's scale pattern. It is very delicate, and if you hold it up to the light, it is almost see-through.

5 A shed skin is longer than the snake itself. This is because the skin stretches as the snake wriggles free.

Snakes on the Move

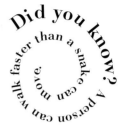

For animals without legs, snakes move around very well. They can glide over or under the ground, climb trees and swim through water. A few snakes can even parachute through the air. Snakes are not speedy – most move at about 3kph (2mph). Their bendy backbones give them a wavy movement. They push themselves along using muscles joined to their ribs. The scales on their skin also grip surfaces to help with movement.

▶ **S-SHAPED MOVER**
Most snakes move in an S-shaped path, pushing the side curves of their bodies backwards against the surface they are moving on or through. The muscular waves of the snake's body hit surrounding objects and the whole body is pushed forward from there.

▼ **CONCERTINA SNAKE**
The green whip snake moves with an action rather like a concertina (see the diagram on the facing page). A concertina is played by squeezing it forwards and backwards.

▲ **SWIMMING SNAKE**
The banded sea snake's stripes stand out as it glides through the water. Snakes swim using S-shaped movements. A sea snake's tail is flattened from side to side to give it extra power, like the oar on a row boat.

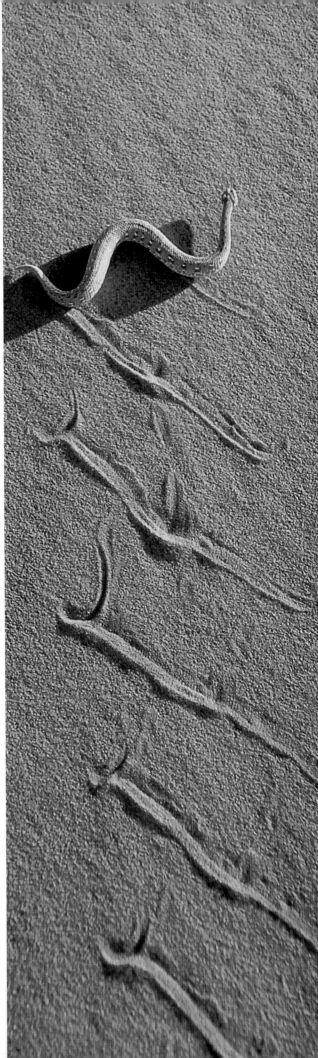

corn snake
(*Elaphe guttata*)

▶ SIDEWINDING
The way snakes that live on loose sand move along is called sidewinding. The snake anchors its head and tail in the sand and throws the middle part of its body sideways.

Did you know? The fastest land snake is the black mamba, moving at up to 11kph (7mph).

▼ HOW SNAKES MOVE
Most land snakes move in four different ways, depending on the type of terrain they are crossing and the type of snake.

1 S-shaped movement: the snake wriggles from side to side.

2 Concertina movement: the snake pulls one half of its body along first, then the other half.

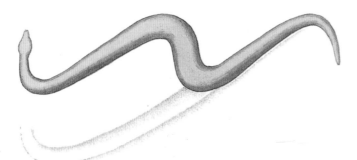

3 Sidewinding movement: the snake throws the middle part of its body forwards, keeping the head and tail on the ground.

4 Caterpillar movement: the snake uses its belly scutes to pull itself along in a straight line.

▲ EYESIGHT

Snakes have no eyelids to cover their eyes. Eyesight varies in snakes, but those with the best eyesight are tree snakes, such as this green mamba, and day hunters such as garter snakes.

Snake Senses

To find prey and avoid enemies, snakes rely more on their senses of smell, taste and touch than on sight and hearing. Snakes have no ears, but they do have one earbone joined at the jaw. The lower jaw picks up sound vibrations moving through the ground. As well as ordinary senses, snakes also have some special ones. They are one of the few animals that taste and smell with their tongues.

▲ NIGHT HUNTER

The horned viper's eyes open wide at night (*above*). During the day, its pupils close to narrow slits (*below*).

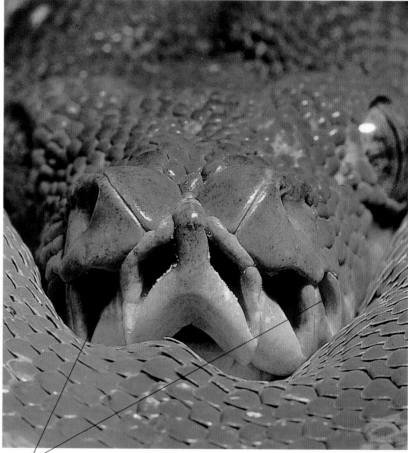

heat pits

▲ SENSING HEAT

The green tree python senses heat given off by its prey through pits on the sides of its face. These heat sensors are lined with nerves. They allow a snake to find and kill prey even in total darkness.

◄ **THE FORKED TONGUE**

When a snake wants to investigate its surroundings, it flicks its tongue to taste the air. The forked tongue picks up tiny chemical particles of scent.

▲ **HEARING**

As it has no ears, the cobra cannot hear the music played by the snake charmer. It follows the movements of the pipe, which resemble a snake, and rises up as it prepares to defend itself.

► **JACOBSON'S ORGAN**

As a snake draws its tongue back into its mouth, it presses the forked tip into the two openings of the Jacobson's organ. This organ is in the roof of the mouth and it analyses tastes and smells.

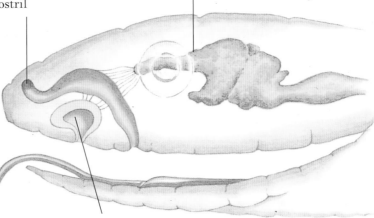

nostril

brain

Jacobson's organ

17

Food and Hunting

Snakes eat different foods and hunt in different ways depending on their size, their species and where they live. Some snakes eat a wide variety of food, while others have a more specialized diet. A snake has to make the most of each meal because it moves fairly slowly and does not get the chance to catch prey very often. A snake's body works at a slow rate so it can go for months without eating.

▲ TREE HUNTERS
A rat snake grasps a baby bluebird in its jaws and begins the process of digestion. Rat snakes often slither up trees in search of baby birds, eggs or squirrels.

rat snake
(*Elaphe*)

▲ FISHY FOOD
The tentacled snake lives on fish. It probably hides among plants in the water and grabs fish as they swim past.

▼ TRICKY LURE
The Australasian death adder's bright tail tip looks like a worm. The adder wriggles the 'worm' to lure lizards, birds and small mammals to come within its range.

◄ EGG-EATERS

The African egg-eater snake checks an egg with its tongue to make sure it is fresh. Then it swallows the egg whole. It uses the pointed ends of the bones in its backbone to crack the eggshell. It eats the egg and coughs up the crushed shell.

► SURPRISE ATTACK

Lunch for this gaboon viper is a mouse! The gaboon viper hides among dry leaves on the forest floor. Its pattern and markings make it very difficult to spot. It waits for a small animal to pass by, then grabs hold of its prey in a surprise attack. Many other snakes that hunt by day also ambush their prey.

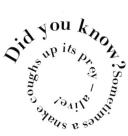

Did you know? Sometimes a snake coughs up its prey – alive!

smooth snake
(*Coronella austriaca*)

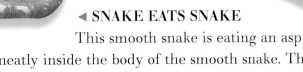

◄ SNAKE EATS SNAKE

This smooth snake is eating an asp viper. The viper fits neatly inside the body of the smooth snake. This makes it easier to swallow than animals that are different shapes.

Teeth and Jaws

Most snakes have short, sharp teeth that are good for gripping and holding prey, but not for chewing it into smaller pieces. The teeth are not very strong, and often get broken, so they are continually being replaced. Venomous snakes also have some larger teeth called fangs. When the snake bites, venom flows down the fangs to paralyse the prey and break down its body. All snakes swallow their prey head-first and whole. Special loose jaws allow the snake to open its mouth very wide.

▼ BACK FANGS

A few venomous snakes have fangs at the back of their mouths. This African boomslang is digging its fangs hard into a chameleon's flesh to get enough venom inside.

▲ OPEN WIDE

An eyelash viper opens its mouth as wide as possible to scare an enemy. Its fangs are folded back against the roof of the mouth. When it attacks, the fangs swing forwards.

viper skull

movable fangs

▲ FOLDING FANGS

Vipers and elapid snakes have fangs at the front of the mouth. A viper's long fangs can fold back. When it strikes, the fangs swing forward to stick out in front of the mouth.

upper jaw

hinge

lower jaw

teeth

python skull

▲ STRETCHY JAWS

When a snake eats, a hinge at the back of the lower jaw lets the jaw swing wide, like a gate. The lower jaw is in two halves connected by a stretchy ligament, so the jaw can stretch sideways, and the two sides of the jaw can move separately. One side holds the prey, while the other side slides forward to get a new grip.

▲ SIMPLE TEETH

A python is not a venomous snake, so it does not have fangs. The teeth curve backwards to help the python keep hold of its prey. A snake's teeth are attached to the inner edges of the jawbones rather than on top of them.

cobra skull

fixed fangs

► FRONT FANGS

All elapid snakes, such as cobras, mambas, coral snakes and sea kraits, are front fanged. Their short, fixed fangs do not move. Muscles contract to pump venom into the snake's prey.

Did you know? The gaboon viper has the longest fangs of any snake.

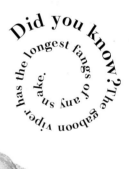

21

Stranglers and Poisoners

Most snakes kill their prey before eating it. Snakes kill by using venom or by squeezing their prey to death. Snakes that squeeze, called constrictors, stop their prey from breathing. Victims die from suffocation or shock. To swallow living or dead prey, a snake opens its jaws wide. Lots of slimy saliva helps the meal to slide down. After eating, a snake yawns widely to put its jaws back into place. Digestion can take several days, or even weeks.

American racer
(*Coluber constrictor*)

▲ BIG MOUTHFUL

This American racer is trying to swallow a living frog. The frog has puffed up its body with air to make it more difficult for the snake to swallow.

▲ AT FULL STRETCH

This fer-de-lance snake is at full stretch to swallow its huge meal. It is a large pit viper that kills with venom.

▲ SWALLOWING A MEAL

The copperhead, a venomous snake from North America, holds on to a dead mouse.

▲ KILLING TIME

A crocodile is slowly squeezed to death by a rock python. The time it takes for a constricting snake to kill its prey depends on the size of the prey and how strong it is.

Did you know? King cobras sometimes kill Indian elephants by biting them on the trunk.

► COILED KILLER

The spotted python sinks its teeth into its victim. It throws coils around the victim's body, and tightens its grip until the animal cannot breathe.

spotted python
(*Liasis maculosus*)

▼ BREATHING TUBE

An African python shows its breathing tube. As the snake eats, the windpipe moves to the front of the mouth so that air can get to and from the lungs.

▲ HEAD-FIRST

A whiptail wallaby's legs disappear inside a carpet python's body. Snakes usually try to swallow their prey head-first so that legs, wings or scales fold back. This helps the victim to slide into the snake's stomach more easily.

1 Rat snakes feed on rats, mice, voles, lizards, birds and eggs. Many of them hunt at night. They are good climbers and can even go up trees with smooth bark and no branches. Rat snakes find their prey by following a scent trail or waiting to ambush an animal.

Let's Do Lunch!

This rat snake is using its strong coils to kill a vole. Rodents, such as voles and rats, are a rat snake's preferred food. With the vole held tightly in its teeth, the snake coils around its body. It squeezes hard to stop the vole breathing. When the vole is dead, the rat snake swallows its meal head-first.

2 When the rat snake is near enough to its prey, it strikes quickly. Its sharp teeth sink into the victim's body to stop it running or flying away. The snake then loops its coils around the victim as fast as possible, before the animal can bite or scratch to defend itself.

3 Each time the vole breathes out, the rat snake squeezes harder around its rib cage to stop the vole breathing in again. Breathing becomes more difficult and soon the victim dies from suffocation.

24

4 Once the victim is dead, the rat snake loosens its coils and begins the process of swallowing. It unhinges its jaws and 'walks' its mouth over its meal. The loose lower jaw stretches sideways to fit around the shape of the dead prey.

5 The rat snake swallows its meal head-first. As the vole moves down the snake's throat, its legs fold back against the sides of its body. The way the fur lies makes the vole easier to swallow. The snake's skin stretches as the meal moves down its body.

6 As the vole moves further down inside the snake's body, the skin stretches more. The ribs move apart at the front to make space for the vole's body. The snake pushes its windpipe to the front of its mouth, so that it can use it like a snorkel for breathing. It may take only one or two gulps for a snake to swallow a small animal whole.

Venomous Snakes

Only about 700 species of snake are venomous. Snake poison, called venom, is useful for snakes because it allows them to kill without having to fight a long battle against their prey. Some snake venom works on the prey's body, softening it and making it easier to digest. There are two main kinds of venom. One type attacks the blood and muscles. The other attacks the nervous system, stopping the heart and lungs from working.

spitting cobra
(*Hemachatus haemachatus*)

▲ DEADLY BITE

A copperhead gets ready to strike. Venomous snakes use their sharp fangs to inject a lethal cocktail of chemicals into their prey. The death of victims often occurs in seconds or minutes, depending on the size of prey and where it was bitten.

▼ WARNING ENEMIES

The bright and bold stripes of coral snakes warn predators that they are extremely venomous. There are more than 50 species of coral snake, all with similar patterns. But predators remember the basic pattern and avoid all coral snakes.

▲ VENOM SPIT

Spitting cobras have an opening in their fangs to squirt venom into an enemy's face. They aim at the eyes, and the venom can cause blindness.

coral snake
(*Micruroides euryxanthus*)

Did you know? The most venomous snake in the world is the black-headed sea snake.

▲ FANGS FORWARD

The copperhead is a viper, so its fangs swing down from the roof of the mouth, ready to stab its prey. The muscles around the venom glands squeeze venom through the fangs.

copperhead
(*Agkistrodon contortrix*)

Bible Snake

At the beginning of the Bible, a snake is the cause of problems in the Garden of Eden. God told Adam and Eve never to eat fruit from the tree of knowledge of good and evil. However, the snake persuaded Eve to eat the fruit. It told Eve that the fruit would make her as clever as God. Eve gave some fruit to Adam too. As a punishment, Adam and Eve had to leave the Garden of Eden and lose the gift of eternal life.

▲ MILKING VENOM
Venom is collected from a black mamba.

green bush viper
(*Atheris squamigera*)

Focus on Vipers

Vipers are the most efficient venomous snakes of all. Their long fangs can inject venom deep into a victim. The venom acts mainly on the blood and muscles of the prey. Vipers usually have short, thick bodies and triangular heads covered with small, ridged scales. There are two main groups of vipers. Pit vipers have large heat pits on the face, and other vipers do not.

TREE VIPER

The green bush viper lives in tropical forests, mainly in the trees. Its green appearance means that it is well camouflaged against the green leaves. It lies in wait for its prey and then kills it with a quick bite. Once the prey has been caught, the snake must hold tight to stop it falling out of the tree.

BALLOON SNAKE

When threatened, the puff adder swells up like a long balloon. It does this by taking a lot of air into its lungs. Being larger makes it look even more dangerous. Puff adders also hiss loudly.

puff adder
(*Bitis arietans*)

rattlesnake
(*Crotalus*)

QUICK JAB

This rattlesnake is exploring its surroundings with its forked tongue. When the rattlesnake strikes at its prey, the hinged fangs swing forward and lock into place. The viper gives its prey a quick injection of venom, then lets go. The prey soon dies, so there is no need for the snake to hold on to it.

HEAT DETECTORS

This Sumatran pit viper has a large heat pit on each side of its head, between the nostril and the eye. The heat pit is larger than the nostril. It can detect the heat given off by warm-blooded prey. By turning its head from side to side, a pit viper can work out the direction of its prey.

Sumatran pit viper
(*Trimeresurus sumatranus*)

SLOW SNAKE

Asp vipers are slow-moving snakes. They are active both by day and by night. Their main sources of food are mice, lizards and baby birds.

29

Avoiding Enemies

The predators of snakes include birds of prey, foxes, racoons, mongooses, baboons, crocodiles, frogs and even other snakes. If they are in danger, snakes usually prefer to hide or escape. Many come out to hunt at night, when it is more difficult for predators to catch them. If they cannot escape, snakes often make themselves look big and fierce, hiss loudly or strike at their enemies. Some pretend to be dead. Giving off a horrible smell is another good way of getting rid of an enemy!

▶ **SMELLY SNAKE**
The cottonmouth is named after its mouth, which is white inside. If it is attacked, it opens its mouth to threaten enemies and it can also give off a strong-smelling liquid from near the tail.

◀ **EAGLE ENEMY**
The short-toed eagle uses its powerful toes to catch snakes. It eats large snakes on the ground. It carries small snakes back to the nest to feed its chicks.

vine snake
(*Oxybelis fulgidus*)

◀ **SCARY MOUTH**
Like many snakes, this vine snake opens its mouth very wide to startle predators. The inside of the mouth is bright red and warns off the predator. If the predator does not go away, the snake will give a venomous bite with the fangs at the back of the mouth.

► PLAYING DEAD

This grass snake knows that most predators prefer healthy, living prey. So it protects itself by pretending to be dead. It rolls on to its back, opens its mouth and keeps quite still.

cottonmouth
(*Agkistrodon piscivorus*)

◄ DRAMATIC DISPLAY

The hognose snake is harmless, but can make itself look dangerous. It flattens its neck to make a hood. It hisses loudly and strikes towards the enemy. Then it smears itself with smelly scent.

► HIDDEN SNAKE

The horned viper buries itelf so that it cannot be seen by its enemies.

▲ LOOKING LARGER

The cobra spreads its hood wide to make itself look too big to swallow.

31

HOOD VARIETY

Like spitting cobras, the king cobra and the water cobra, this Egyptian cobra has a narrow hood. The Indian cobra and the Cape cobra of southern Africa have much wider hoods. The Egyptian cobra ranges over much of Africa and into Arabia.

HOOD PATTERNS

Some cobras have eyespots on the back of their hoods to make them look more scary.

THE HOOD

The cobra's hood is made from flaps of skin supported by long ribs. Mostly, the skin rests flat against the body. But when it is alarmed the cobra spreads its neck ribs, stretching the neck skin to form a hood.

Focus on the Cobra and its Relatives

Cobras are highly venomous snakes. Some of them can squirt deadly venom at their enemies. Cobra venom works mainly on the nervous system, causing breathing or heart problems. Cobras are members of the elapid snake family, which includes the African mambas, the coral snakes of the Americas and all the venomous snakes of Australia.

LARGE COBRA
The king cobra is the largest venomous snake, growing to a length of 5.5m (18ft). King cobras are the only snakes known to build a nest. The female guards her eggs and hatchlings until they leave the nest.

MIND THE MAMBA
The green mamba lives in trees. Other mambas, such as the black mamba, live mostly on the ground. Mambas are slim, long snakes that can grow up to 4m (13ft) long. Their venom is very powerful and can kill a person in only ten minutes!

DO NOT DISTURB!
The Australian mainland tiger snake is a member of the elapid snake family. It is the world's fourth most venomous snake. If it is disturbed, it puffs up its body, flattens its neck and hisses loudly. The diet of these snakes includes fish, frogs, birds and small mammals.

33

rainbow boa
(*Epicrates cenchria*)

◄ **CHANGING HUES**
◄ **CHANGING HUES**
The rainbow boa is iridescent. Light is made up of all the hues of the rainbow. When light hits the thin outer layer of the snake's scales, it splits into different shades. What we see depends on the type of scales and the way light bounces off them.

Patterns and Camouflage

Snakes get their patterns from the pigments in the scales and from the way light reflects off the scales. Dull shades help to camouflage a snake and hide it from its enemies. Brighter markings startle predators or warn them that a snake is venomous. Harmless snakes sometimes copy the markings of venomous snakes. Darker pigments may help snakes to absorb heat during cooler weather. Young snakes can look different from their parents, but no one knows why.

milk snake
(*Lampropeltis doliata*)

Did you know? Milk snakes always have black bands between the red and yellow – coral snakes have the red and yellow touching.

ring-necked snake
(*Diadophis punctatus*)

◄ **BRIGHT PATTERNS**
This snake's red tail draws attention away from the most vital part of its body – the head.

◄ COPYCAT

The bright red, yellow and black bands of this milk snake copy the appearance of the venomous coral snake. The milk snake is not venomous, but predators leave it alone – just in case! This is found in milk snakes in the southeast of the USA.

▼ ALBINO SNAKES

White snakes are called albinos. In the wild, these snakes stand out against the background and are usually killed by predators before they can reproduce.

▼ SNAKE MARKINGS

Many snakes are marked with striking patches. These markings are usually caused by groups of different pigments in the scales.

red-tailed boa
(*Boa constrictor*)

◄ CLEVER CAMOUFLAGE

Among the dead leaves of the rainforest floor, the gaboon viper becomes almost invisible. Many snakes have patterns that match their surroundings.

35

Reproduction

Snakes do not live as families, and parents do not look after their young. Males and females come together to mate, and pairs may stay together for the breeding season. Most snakes are ready to mate when they are between two and five years old. In cooler climates, snakes usually mate in spring so that their young have time to feed and grow before the winter starts. In tropical climates, snakes often mate before the rainy season, when there is plenty of food for their young. Male snakes find females by following their scent trails.

flowerpot snake
(*Typhlops braminus*)

▲ **NO MATE**
Scientists believe that female flowerpot snakes can produce young without males. This is useful when they move to new areas, as one snake can start a new colony. However, all the young are the same, and if conditions change, the snakes cannot adapt and may die out.

▶ **FIGHTING**
Male adders fight to test which one is the stronger. They rear up and face each other, then twist their necks together. Each snake tries to push the other to the ground. In the end, one of them gives up.

spur

◀ **SNAKE SPURS**
Both boa and python males have small spurs on their bodies. These are the remains of back legs that have disappeared as snakes have developed over millions of years. A male uses its spur to scratch or tickle the female during courtship, or to fight with other males. Females' spurs are usually smaller.

▲ **WRESTLING MATCH**

These male Indian rat snakes are fighting to see which is the stronger. The winner stands a better chance of mating. The snakes hiss and strike out, but they seldom get hurt.

▶ **SIMILARITIES AND DIFFERENCES**

No one knows why the male and female of the snake shown here have such different head shapes. In fact, male and female snakes of the same species usually look similar because snakes rely on scent rather than sight to find a mate.

male

Madagascar leaf-nosed snake (*Langaha nasuta*)

female

◀ **MATING**

When a female anaconda is ready to mate, she lets the male coil his tail around hers. The male has to place his sperm inside the female's body to fertilize her eggs. The eggs can then develop into baby snakes.

37

Eggs

Some snakes lay eggs and some give birth to fully developed, or live, young. Egg-laying snakes include cobras and pythons. A few weeks after mating, the female looks for a safe, warm, moist place to lay between 6 and 40 eggs. This may be under a rotting log, in sandy soil, under a rock or in a compost heap. Most snakes cover their eggs and leave them to hatch by themselves. A few snakes stay with their eggs to protect them from predators and the weather. However, once the eggs hatch, all snakes abandon their young.

▲ BEACH BIRTH
Sea kraits are the only sea snakes to lay eggs. They often do this in caves, above the water level.

► EGG CARE
This female python has piled up her eggs and coiled herself around them to protect them from predators. The female Indian python twitches her muscles to warm up her body. The extra heat helps the young to develop. Snake eggs need to be kept at a certain temperature if they are to develop properly.

◄ LAYING EGGS
The Oenpellis python lays rounded eggs. The eggs of smaller snakes are usually long and thin to fit inside their smaller body. Some snakes lay long, thin eggs when they are young, but more rounded eggs when they grow larger.

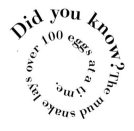

Did you know? The mud snake lays over 100 eggs at a time.

▼ CHILDREN'S PYTHON MASS HATCHING

As they hatch, these children's pythons flatten their egg shells.
A snake's egg shell is leathery, not brittle like the shell of a bird's
egg. Birds' eggs would break into pieces if they were squashed.
A snake's egg is not watertight, so it is
laid in a moist place to stop it
drying up.

children's
pythons
(*Liasis
childreni*)

▼ HIDDEN EGGS

Eggs are hidden from predators in the soil, or under rocks
and logs. Eggs are never completely buried as the young
need to breathe air that flows through the outer shell.

▲ HOT SPOTS

This female grass snake has laid her
eggs in a warm pile of rotting plants.

Focus on Hatching Out

About two to four months after the adults mate, the baby snakes hatch out of their eggs. Inside the egg, the baby snake feeds on the yolk, which is full of goodness. Once the snake has fully developed and the yolk has been used up, the snake is ready to hatch. All the eggs in a clutch tend to hatch at the same time. A few days later, the baby snake wriggles away to start life without any parents.

1 Eight weeks after being laid, these rat snake eggs are hatching. While they developed inside the egg, each baby rat snake fed on its yolk. A day or so before hatching, the yolk sac was drawn inside the snake's body. A small scar, rather like a tummy button, will show where the snake was once joined to the yolk.

2 The baby snake has become restless, twisting inside its shell. It is now fully developed and cannot get enough oxygen through its shell. A snake's egg has an almost watertight shell, but water and gases, such as oxygen, pass in and out of it through tiny holes (pores). As the baby snake prepares to hatch, it cuts a slit in the shell with a sharp egg tooth on its snout. This egg tooth will drop off a few hours after hatching.

3 After it has broken through the stretchy shell, the baby snake has a rest. It pokes its nose through the slit in the egg to breathe the air and take a first look at the strange and exciting world outside.

4 All the eggs in this clutch have hatched at the same time (a clutch is a set of eggs laid by a snake). After making the first slits in their leathery shells, the baby snakes will not crawl out straight away. They poke their heads out of their eggs to taste the air with their forked tongues. If they are disturbed, they will slide back inside the shell where they feel safe. They may stay inside the shell for a few days.

Did you know? Some snakes lay as many as 100 eggs in one clutch.

5 Eventually, the baby snake slithers out of the egg. It may be as much as seven times longer than the egg because it was coiled up inside.

Pope's tree viper (*Trimeresurus popeorum*)

▲ TREE BIRTH

Tree snakes often give birth in the branches. The membrane around each baby snake sticks to the leaves and helps stop the baby from falling out of the branches to the ground.

▲ BIRTH PLACE

This female sand viper has chosen a quiet, remote spot to give birth to her young. Snakes usually give birth in a hidden place, where the young are safe from enemies.

Giving Birth

Some snakes give birth to fully developed or live young, instead of laying eggs. Snakes that do this include boas, rattlesnakes, adders and most sea snakes. The eggs develop inside the mother's body surrounded by see-through bags, called membranes. While the baby snake is developing inside the mother, it gets its food from the yolk of the egg. The babies are born after a delivery that may last for hours. Anything from 6 to 50 babies are born at a time. At birth, they are still inside their membranes.

▶ BABY BAGS

These red-tailed boas have just been born. They are still inside their see-through bags. The bags are made of a clear, thin, tough membrane, rather like the one inside the shell of a hen's egg.

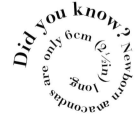

Did you know? Newborn anacondas are only 6cm (2½in) long.

▶ BREAKING FREE

This baby rainbow boa has just pushed
its head through its surrounding
membrane. Snakes have to break free
of their baby bags on their own. Each
baby has an egg tooth to cut a slit in
the membrane and wriggle out. The
babies usually do this a few seconds
after birth.

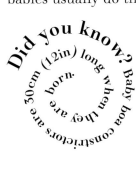

Did you know? Baby boa constrictors are 30cm (12in) long when they are born.

◀ NEW BABY

A red-tailed boa
has broken free
of its baby bag,
or egg sac, which
is in the front of
the picture. The
baby's appearance
is bright. Some
newborn babies
crawl off straight
away, while others
stay with their
mother for a
few days.

◀ TURNING GREEN

This vivid red baby is an emerald
tree boa. As it grows up, it will
turn green. Although boas
and pythons are very similar
snakes in some ways, one of
the main differences between
them is that boas give birth
to live young while
pythons lay eggs.

Did you know? Timber rattlesnake mothers defend their newborn babies for a few days.

**emerald
tree boa**
(*Epicrates
cenchria*)

Growth and Development

The size of baby snakes when they are born or when they hatch from their eggs, how much they eat and the climate around them all affect their rate of growth. In warm climates, snakes may double or triple their length in just one year. Some snakes are mature and almost fully grown after three to five years, but slow growth may continue throughout their lives. Young snakes shed their skin more often than adults because they are growing quickly. While they are growing, young snakes are easy prey for animals such as birds, racoons, toads and rats.

▼ FAST FOOD

Like all young snakes, this Burmese python must eat as much as possible in order to grow quickly. Young snakes eat smaller prey than their parents, such as ants, earthworms and flies.

▲ DEADLY BABY

This baby European adder can give a nasty bite soon after hatching. Luckily, its venom is not very strong.

mother European adder

baby European adder

▲ MOTHER AND BABY

European adders give birth in summer. The young must grow fast so that they are big enough to survive winter hibernation.

Burmese python
(*Python molurus
bivittatus*)

Heracles the Strong

Heracles was the son of Zeus, king of the ancient Greek gods. His mother was Alcmene, an ordinary human being. Zeus's wife, Hera, was jealous of Alcmene's baby. She sent two venomous snakes to kill Heracles as he slept. But Heracles was strong and killed the snakes by strangling them with his bare hands.

rattlesnake
(*Crotalus*)   short rattle

▲ DIET CHANGE

Many young Amazon tree boas live on islands in the West Indies. They start off by feeding on lizards, but as they grow they switch to feeding on birds and mammals.

► RATTLE AGE

You cannot tell the age of a rattlesnake by counting the sections of its rattle because several sections may be added each year and pieces of the rattle may break off.

Where Snakes Live

Snakes live on every continent except Antarctica. They are most common in deserts and rainforests. They cannot survive in very cold places because they use the heat around them to make their bodies work. This is why most snakes live in warm places where the temperature is high enough for them to stay active day and night. In cooler places, snakes may spend the cold winter months asleep. This is called hibernation.

▲ **GRASSLANDS**
The European grass snake is one of the few snakes to live on grasslands, where there is little food or shelter.

◄ **MOUNTAINS**
The Pacific rattlesnake is sometimes found in the mountains of the western USA, often on the lower slopes covered with loose rock. In general, though, mountains are problem places for snakes because of their cold climates.

▲ **WINTER SLEEP**
Thousands of garter snakes emerge after their winter sleep. Snakes often hibernate in caves or underground, where it is warmer.

▼ TROPICAL RAINFORESTS

The greatest variety of snakes lives in tropical rainforests, including this Brazilian rainbow boa. There is plenty to eat, from insects, birds and bats to frogs.

▲ LIVING IN TREES

The eyelash viper lives in the Central American rainforest. The climate in rainforests is warm all year round, so snakes can stay active all the time. There are also plenty of places to live – in trees, on the forest floor, in soil and in rivers.

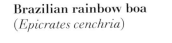

Brazilian rainbow boa
(*Epicrates cenchria*)

► BURROWERS

Yellow-headed worm snakes live under tree bark. Many worm, or thread, snakes live under ground where the soil is warm.

◄ DESERTS

This African puff adder lives in the Kalahari desert of southern Africa. Many snakes live in deserts because they can survive with little food and water.

47

Tree Snakes

With their long, thin, flat bodies and pointed heads, tree snakes slide easily through the branches of tropical forests. Some can even glide from tree to tree. Tree boas and pythons have ridges on their belly scales to give them extra gripping power. Many tree snakes also have long, thin tails that coil tightly around branches. Green or brown camouflage patterns keep tree snakes well hidden among the leaves and branches.

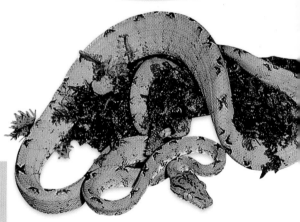

▲ CAMOUFLAGE
This Amazon tree boa has patterns for camouflage. Many tree snakes are green or brown with patterns that break up the outline of their body shape. Some even have patterns that look like mosses and lichens.

▲ TREE TWINS
The green tree python lives in the rainforests of New Guinea. It looks similar to the emerald tree boa and behaves in a similar way, but they are not closely related.

◄ GRASPING
In a rainforest in Costa Rica, a blunt-headed tree snake has caught a lizard. It grasps its prey firmly so that it does not fall out of the tree. Tree snakes have long, sharp teeth, good for piercing skin.

long-nosed whip snake
(*Ahaetulla mycterizens*)

▲ HEADS AND EYES

The long-nosed whip snake opens its
bright mouth to scare away a predator.
It has a long head, with a pointed snout – an
ideal shape for sliding through branches.

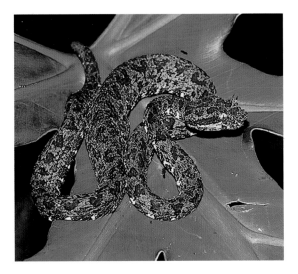

Cook's tree boa
(*Boa cookii*)

▲ VIPER REFLEXES

The green eyelash viper has such
speedy reflexes that it can catch birds
as they fly through the trees. It has to
hold on to its prey while its venom
takes effect.

▶ BODY WEIGHT

Tree snakes have long, thin,
light bodies. This helps them
to crawl along small branches
without breaking them. They can
also stretch easily from one branch
to another.

49

Focus on the Emerald

With their green coils looped around branches, emerald tree boas lurk among leaves in the rainforests of South America. These tree boas are good climbers, hanging head-first from branches to seize fast-moving prey in their teeth. To rest, they lie with their coils encircling a narrow branch, and their head lying on top.

UPSIDE-DOWN MEALS

To catch a meal, emerald tree boas drape their coils over a horizontal branch and hang their heads down. Once the snake has a firm hold on its prey with its teeth, it coils around its victim. It slowly squeezes with its coils to stop the animal breathing. When the animal is dead, the emerald tree boa swallows it head-first, so that it slides down easily.

CLIMBING SKILLS

Tree boas are longer and slimmer than boas that live on the ground. This helps them to slide through the branches.

GRIPPING

The emerald tree boa's tail grips the branch. As the boa climbs, it reaches up with its front end and coils itself around a branch, then pulls up the rest of its body.

Tree Boa

NEW PIGMENTS
Young emerald tree boas are orange, pink or yellow when they are born. They gradually change to green in their first year by producing new pigments in their skin. No one is sure why the young are different from the adults. They may live in different places from the adults and so need a different appearance for effective camouflage.

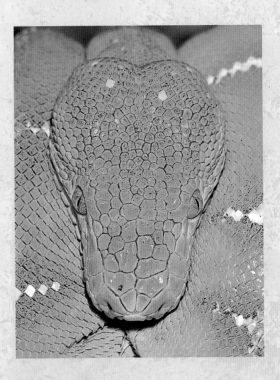

HOT LIPS
Emerald tree boas use pits on their lips to sense the heat given off by prey animals.

LETHAL JAWS
The emerald tree boa can open its mouth very wide to fit more of its prey inside. This is why the snake can feed on animals that move quickly, such as birds.

Desert Snakes

Deserts are full of snakes. This is partly because snakes can survive for a long time without food. They don't need to use energy from food to produce body heat because they get heat energy from their surroundings. It is also because their waterproof skins stop them losing too much water. Snakes push between rocks or down rodent burrows to escape the Sun's heat and the night's bitter cold. Some snakes rest quietly underground during very hot, dry periods.

◄ SCALE SOUNDS

If threatened, the desert horned viper makes a loud rasping sound by rubbing together jagged scales along the sides of its body. This warns predators to keep away.

horned viper
(*Cerastes cerastes*)

► RATTLING
A rattlesnake shakes its rattle to warn enemies to keep away. It shakes its tail and often lifts its head off the ground. It cannot hear the buzzing noise it makes – but its enemies can.

▶ SAND SHUFFLE

The desert horned viper shuffles under the sand by rocking its body to and fro. It spreads its ribs to flatten its body and pushes its way down until it almost disappears. It strikes out at its prey from this position.

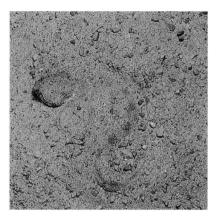

◀ SIDEWINDING

Many desert snakes, such as this Peringuey's viper, travel in a movement called sidewinding. As the snake moves, only a small part of its body touches the hot sand at any time. Sidewinding also helps to stop the snake sinking down into the loose sand.

◀ HIDDEN BOA

The patterns of this sand boa make it hard for predators and prey to spot among desert rocks and sand. The sand boa's long, round body shape helps it to burrow down into the sand.

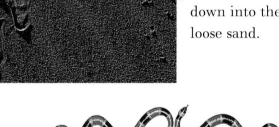

The Hopi Indians

This Native North American was a Hopi snake chief. The Hopi people used snakes in their rain dances to carry prayers to the rain gods to make rain fall on their desert lands.

Water Snakes

Some snakes live in marshy areas or at the edge of freshwater lakes and rivers. Two groups of snakes live in salty sea water. They breathe air, but they can stay underwater for a long time. Glands on their heads get rid of some of the salt from the water. Sea snakes have hollow front fangs and are very venomous. This is because a sea snake has to subdue its prey quickly in order to avoid losing it in the depths of the sea.

◄ SEA SENSES

A sea snake's eyes and nostrils lie towards the top of the head. This means it can take a breath without lifting its head right out of the water, and the eyes can watch out for predators about to attack.

▼ CHAMPION SWIMMER

Northern water snakes are good swimmers, rarely found far from fresh water. They feed mainly on fish, frogs, salamanders and toads. At the first sign of danger, they dive under the water.

► BREATH CONTROL

Sea snakes have a large lung enabling them to stay underwater for a few hours.

◄ **HEAVY WEIGHT**
The green anaconda lurks in swamps and slow-moving rivers, waiting for birds, turtles and caimans to come within reach of its strong coils. Green anacondas weigh up to 227kg (500lb)!

sea krait
(*Laticauda colubrina*)

▲ **LAND LUBBER**
The sea krait is less well adapted to the water and lays eggs on land.

55

Snake Families

Scientists have divided the 2,700 different kinds of snake into about ten groups, called families. These are the colubrids, the elapids, the vipers, the boas and pythons, the sea snakes, the sunbeam snakes, the blind snakes and worm snakes, the thread snakes, the shieldtail snakes and the false coral snake.

The snakes in each family have features in common. The biggest family is the colubrid family, with over 1,800 different species of snake.

Did you know? The viper family includes rattlesnakes, adders, asps and pit vipers.

▲ **COLUBRIDS**

About three-quarters of all the world's snakes, including this milk snake, belong to the colubrid family. Most colubrids are not venomous. They have no left lung or hip bones.

▲ **VIPERS**

Snakes in this family, such as the sand viper, have long, hollow fangs that can be folded back inside the mouth when they are not needed.

► **ELAPIDS**

Elapids, such as this cobra, are venomous snakes that live in hot countries. They have short, fixed fangs at the front of their mouths.

Indian cobra
(*Naja naja*)

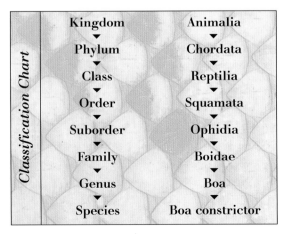

Classification Chart	Kingdom	Animalia
	▼	▼
	Phylum	Chordata
	▼	▼
	Class	Reptilia
	▼	▼
	Order	Squamata
	▼	▼
	Suborder	Ophidia
	▼	▼
	Family	Boidae
	▼	▼
	Genus	Boa
	▼	▼
	Species	Boa constrictor

This chart shows how a boa constrictor is classified within the animal kingdom.

Colombian rainbow boa
(*Epicrates cenchria maurus*)

▶

BOAS AND PYTHONS

This family includes snakes that kill by constriction rather than poisoning. They have curved teeth, hip bones and tiny back leg bones.

▶ **SEA SNAKES**

Some sea snakes are born in the sea and spend all their lives there, and others spend part of their time on land. Sea snakes have flattened tails for swimming and nostrils that can be closed off under the water. Most live in warm waters, from the Red Sea to New Zealand and Japan.

◀ **SUNBEAM SNAKES**

The two members of the sunbeam family are burrowing snakes that live in South-east Asia and southern China. Unlike most other snakes, they have two working lungs, though the left one is about half the size of the right.

57

Snake Relatives

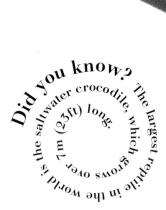

sand lizard

Snakes are part of a large group of animals called reptiles. There are about 6,000 different kinds of reptiles, nearly half of which are snakes. Other reptiles include turtles and tortoises, lizards, crocodiles and alligators. Reptiles have bony skeletons with a backbone and bodies covered in scales. They lay eggs with waterproof shells or give birth to live young. Young reptiles look like copies of their parents. Reptiles are cold-blooded and rely on their surroundings for heat, so they live mostly in warm places.

▲ LIZARDS
This sand lizard is threatening an enemy by making itself look big and scary. Lizards have movable eyelids and good eyesight. Most lizards have pointed tongues.

Did you know? The largest reptile in the world is the saltwater crocodile, which grows over 7m (23ft) long.

baby crocodile

◄ CARING CROCODILES
Crocodiles are dangerous reptiles. Yet female crocodiles make doting mothers. They guard their eggs and protect their young until they can fend for themselves.

◀ LEGLESS LIZARDS

Some burrowing lizards have tiny legs – or none at all. Snakes possibly developed from burrowing lizards, which did not need legs for sliding through soil.

Did you know? The only two venomous lizards are the Gila monster and the Mexican bearded lizard.

water dragon

▼ LIZARD TAILS

Lizards, like this water dragon, generally have long tails and shed their skin in several pieces.

▼ TORTOISES

A tortoise has a shell as well as a skeleton. The shell is made from bony plates fused to the ribs, with an outer covering of horny plates. It is useful for protection, but it is also very heavy.

▼ BURROWING LIZARD

Worm lizards dig burrows underground with their strong, hard heads. Their nostrils close during burrowing so they do not get clogged up with soil.

tortoise

worm lizard

59

Conservation

Some snakes are killed because people are afraid of them. Farmers often kill snakes to protect their farm animals and workers, although many snakes actually help farmers by eating pests. In some countries snakes are killed for food or used to make medicines. To help snakes survive, people need to take action to preserve their habitats, so that snakes can live in safety.

▲ FINDING OUT MORE
Scientists use an antenna to pick up radio signals from a transmitter fitted to a rattlesnake. This allows them to track the snake even when they cannot see it. The more we can learn about snakes, the easier it is to protect them.

▲ TROPHY
There are still those who shoot snakes for recreation. The hunters put the snake's rattle or head on display as a trophy demonstrating their sporting achievements.

▶ SNAKES IN DANGER
Snakes, such as this Dumeril's boa, are in danger of dying out. Threats include people taking them from the wild and road building in places where they live.

▲ USING SNAKE SKINS

Snake skins have been used for many years to make souvenirs. Some species have declined as a result of intensive killing for skins in some areas. Recently, countries such as Sri Lanka and India have banned the export of snake skins.

▼ ROUND-UP

This show in North America demonstrates the skill of capturing a rattlesnake. Today rattlesnake hunts are not as common as they once were.

Did you know? Legend says St Patrick banished snakes from Ireland to rid the country of evil.

▼ PET SNAKES

Some people like to keep pet snakes. However, they can do very little and are not happy in captivity. Snakes can lose the ability to hunt and dislike being kept in a confined space.

GLOSSARY

aestivation
A period of rest during heat and drought, similar to hibernation.

albino
An animal that lacks coloration on all or part of its body and which belongs to a species that is usually coloured.

anaconda
A type of boa.

antivenin
A substance made from the blood of mammals and/or snake venom that is used to treat snakebite.

arid
Very dry.

bask
To lie in the warmth of the sun.

boas
A group of snakes that live mainly in North and South America. They kill by constriction and give birth to live young.

brille
A transparent scale covering a snake's eye. It is also called a spectacle.

camouflage
Shades or patterns that help an animal blend into its surroundings.

carnivore
An animal that eats only meat or fish.

classification
Grouping of animals according to their similarities and differences in order to study them. This also suggests how they may have developed over time.

cloaca
Combined opening of the end of the gut, the reproductive system and the urinary system in reptiles, amphibians and birds.

clutch
The number of eggs laid by a female at one time.

cobras
Venomous snakes in the elapid family, with short, fixed fangs at the front of the mouth.

cold-blooded
An animal whose temperature varies with that of its surroundings.

colubrids
Mostly harmless snakes. These snakes make up the biggest group – nearly three-quarters of the world's snakes.

compost heap
A pile of layers of garden plants, leaves and soil. Compost gives off heat as it rots down and can eventually be dug into the soil to make it rich. This helps plants to grow.

constrictor
A snake that kills by coiling its body tightly around its prey to suffocate it.

digestion
The process of absorbing food into the stomach and bowels.

ectotherm
A cold-blooded animal.

egg tooth
A small tooth sticking out of the mouth of snake hatchlings, which is used to slit open the egg.

elapids
A group of venomous snakes that includes the cobras, mambas and the coral snakes. Elapids live in hot countries.

endangered
A species that is at risk of becoming extinct.

epidermis
The outer layer of the skin.

evolution
The process by which living things adapt over generations to changes in their surroundings.

extinct
When every member of a species of animal or plant is dead.

fang
A long, pointed tooth that may be used to deliver venom.

herbivore
An animal that eats only plants.

hibernation
A period of rest during the winter when body processes slow down.

Jacobson's organ
Nerve pits in the roof of a snake's mouth into which the tongue places scent particles.

keratin
A horny substance that makes up a snake's scales.

sections
at the end
of the tail.

mature
Developed enough to be capable
of reproduction.

membrane
A thin film, skin or layer.

moulting
The process by which a snake sheds
its skin.

omnivore
An animal that eats plants and meat.

pigment
Coloured matter in the skin.

pits
Heat sensors located on either side
of a snake's head.

predator
A living thing that catches and kills
other living things for food.

prey
An animal that is hunted by
animals or by people for food.

python
A group of snakes that lives mainly
in Australia, Africa and Asia.
Pythons kill their prey by
constriction. They lay eggs.

rainforest
A tropical forest where it is hot and
wet all year round.

rattlesnakes
Snakes that live mainly in the south-
west United States and Mexico. They
have a warning rattle made of empty

saliva
A colourless liquid produced by
glands in the mouth. Saliva helps to
slide food from the mouth to the
throat. In some snakes, saliva also
aids digestion.

spurs
Leg bones attached to the hip bones,
which are found in boas and pythons
and used during courtship displays.

venom
Poisonous fluid produced in the
glands of certain snakes in order to
kill their prey.

vipers
A group of very venomous snakes
with fangs that fold. Some vipers
have heat pits on their faces. Most
vipers give birth to live young.

warm-blooded
An animal (such as a mouse or a
human being) that is able to maintain
its body at roughly the same
temperature all the time.

warning colours
Bright patterns that show others that
an animal is poisonous or venomous.
Bright shades also warn predators to
keep away.

windpipe
The tube leading from the mouth to
the lungs. It is through this that an
animal takes in fresh air (containing
oxygen) and gives out used air
(containing carbon dioxide).

yolk
Food material that is rich in
protein and fats. It nourishes a
developing embryo inside an egg.

Picture Acknowledgements
l = left, r = right, m = middle
t = top, b = bottom

Jane Burton/Warren Photographic: pages
29m, 40–1 and 48tr; Bruce Coleman Ltd:
pages 6bl, 8bl, 14br, 15r, 16tl, 17tl, 18tl,
19mr, 20ml, 20tr, 20br, 21tr, 21bl, 22br, 27br,
28t, 29b, 30br, 31t, 33mr, 33bl, 33r, 34bl,
36m, 37bl, 39br, 44ml, 44br, 46bl, 46br, 48tr,
48mr, 48b, 50mr, 50b, 53tr, 54bl, 56bl, 56mr,
59br, 60tr and 61b; Ecoscene: pages 17mr and
59tl; Mary Evans Picture Library: pages 45tr
and 53br; FLPA: pages 11mr, 11ml, 16m,
18bl, 23tl, 23tr, 26tl, 26m, 31mr, 32-33, 35tr,
35bl, 38mr, 39t, 39bl, 40–1, 43tr, 45ml, 45br,
48ml, 51bl, 50–1, 52b, 52r, 55tl, 57bl and
60br; Holt Studios International: pages 22tl,
46tr and 58tl; Nature Photographers: page
30bm; NHPA: pages 7bl, 8tl, 9tr, 9bl, 11tl,
14tl, 18br, 19tl, 19br, 22bl, 23bl, 23br, 31ml,
36–7, 37tr, 37mr, 38bl, 42ml, 47tl, 47ml,
47bl, 49ml, 49r, 50tl, 51t and 53m; Oxford
Scientific Films: pages 6tm, 12–13, 24–5, 42t,
43b and 56br; Planet Earth Pictures: pages
28b, 32ml, 32br, 32tr, 38tr, 42br, 43m, 54tr,
54br, 55mr, 57mr, 60ml, 61tl and 61tr;
Visual Arts Library: pages 5br, 11br and 27bl;
Zefa Pictures: page 51br.

INDEX